Sports in Action

Volleyball
in Action

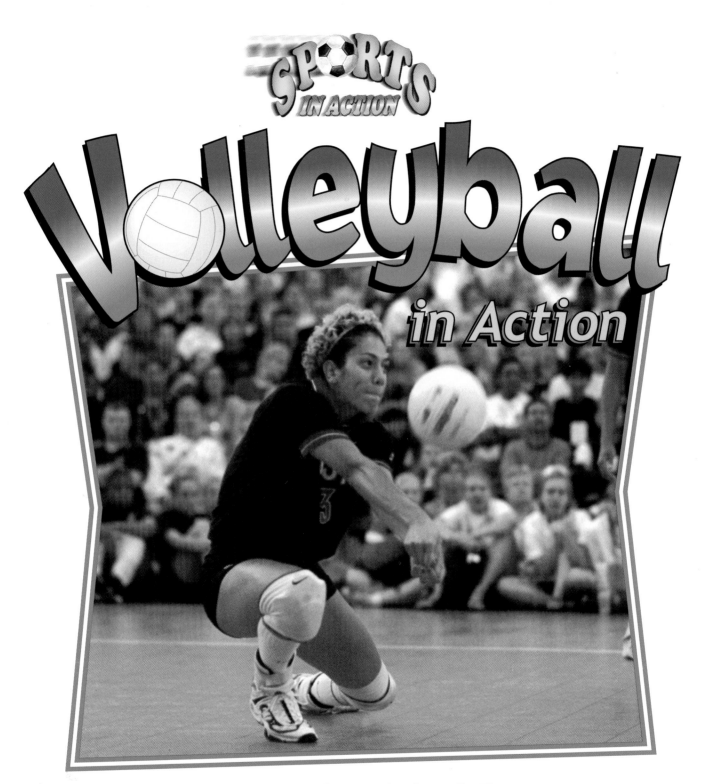

John Crossingham & Sarah Dann

Crabtree Publishing Company

Created by Bobbie Kalman

To Barbara and George Hough, with appreciation and love

Editor-in-Chief
Bobbie Kalman

Writing team
John Crossingham
Sarah Dann
Niki Walker

Managing editor
Lynda Hale

Editors
Kate Calder
Heather Levigne

Computer design
Lynda Hale
Robert MacGregor (cover concept)

Consultant
Scott Koskie,
Captain, Canadian National
Men's Volleyball Team

Special thanks to
Andrew Corolis, Sandy Peters, Anastasia Coutinho, Andrea Hernandez, Suchitra Joshi, Alexandra Newman, Stephanie Wilcox, Katleya Young-Chin, and Ridley College; Marc Crabtree and Blake Malcolm; Glenn Tinley; Jeannine Farley, Luc Tremblay, and Volleyball Canada; Kathy Dosen and USA Volleyball

Every reasonable effort has been made in obtaining authorization, where necessary, to publish images of the athletes who appear in this book. The publishers would be pleased to have any oversights or omissions brought to their attention so that they may be corrected for subsequent printings.

Photographs and reproductions
M. Julian Baum: title page, pages 3, 4, 5, 8, 13, 14, 17, 18, 22, 24, 26; Digital Stock: front cover; Frozen Motion Photography: page 6; Robert Tringali/ SportsChrome: pages 30-31; Volleyball Canada: pages 16, 20, 21, 27, 28

Illustrations
Trevor Morgan: pages 2 (border), 7, 9, 12
Bonna Rouse: back cover, pages 10-11, 15, 16, 17, 19, 21, 23, 25, 27, 29 (right)

Production coordinator and photo researcher
Hannelore Sotzek

Digital prepress
Embassy Graphics

Crabtree Publishing Company

PMB 16A
350 Fifth Avenue,
Suite 3308
New York, NY
10118

360 York Road
RR 4
Niagara-on-the-Lake,
Ontario, Canada
L0S 1J0

73 Lime Walk
Headington,
Oxford
OX3 7AD
United Kingdom

Cataloging in Publication Data
Crossingham, John
    Volleyball in action

(Sports in action)
Includes index.

ISBN 0-7787-0164-6 (library bound) ISBN 0-7787-0176-X (pbk.)
This book introduces the techniques, equipment, rules, and safety requirements of volleyball.

1. Volleyball —Juvenile literature. 2. Volleyball —Training—Juvenile literature. [1. Volleyball.] I. Dann, Sarah, 1970- . II. Title. III. Series: Kalman, Bobbie. Sports in action.

GV1015.3.C76 2000   j796.325   LC 99-38039
                                                          CIP

Contents

What is Volleyball?

Volleyball is a popular sport that is played indoors and outdoors. Two teams of six players stand on either side of a net and **rally**, or hit a volleyball back and forth. Players use mainly their hands and arms to hit the ball over the net. They cannot catch, hold, or carry the ball. The object of the game is to hit the ball over the net so that it lands on the other team's side of the floor. When it hits the ground, a point may be scored.

Point, game, match!

Volleyball competitions are called **matches**. Some matches consist of three **games**, and older players play five-game matches. Games are also known as **sets**. To win the match, a team must win two of three, or three of five, games. In most games the first team to score fifteen points wins. A team must win by at least two points. For example, if one team's score is 14 and the other's is 15, the game continues until one team has two more points than the other.

A game for everyone

Many countries have men's and women's national volleyball teams. They compete in the summer Olympic Games, which are held every four years. Volleyball became an Olympic sport in 1964.

Birth of the game

William G. Morgan invented volleyball in 1895. Originally, the game was called **mintonette**. The name was changed to volleyball because of the way players **volley**, or hit the ball into the air and over the net. The sport quickly became popular with men and women.

Order of the Court

Volleyball is played on a surface called a **court**. A court is divided into two sides by a high net. One team plays on each side, and they switch sides at the end of each game. The court is marked with boundaries called **sidelines** and **end lines**. The area outside these lines is called the **free zone**. A ball that lands in the free zone is **out-of-bounds**. If it lands on a line it is still in play.

Front and back

The **spiking line** or **attack line** divides each side of the court into two sections. The **front court** is the section closest to the net and the **back court** is the section farthest from the net. Three players called **attackers** play in the front court. They hit the ball hard over the net and try to block their opponents' shots. The back-court players receive **serves** and pass the ball to the attackers.

The officials

Officials make sure players follow the rules. All matches have a **referee**, who is the top official. Many games have two referees and two or more **line judges**. Players and coaches cannot argue with an official's **calls**, or decisions. Officials stand in the free zone so that they do not interfere with the match.

Can I play now?

Most teams have more than six players. The extra players are called **substitutes**, or **subs**. The coach puts subs into the match to replace tired or injured players. Subs sit on a bench in the free zone and cheer on their teammates.

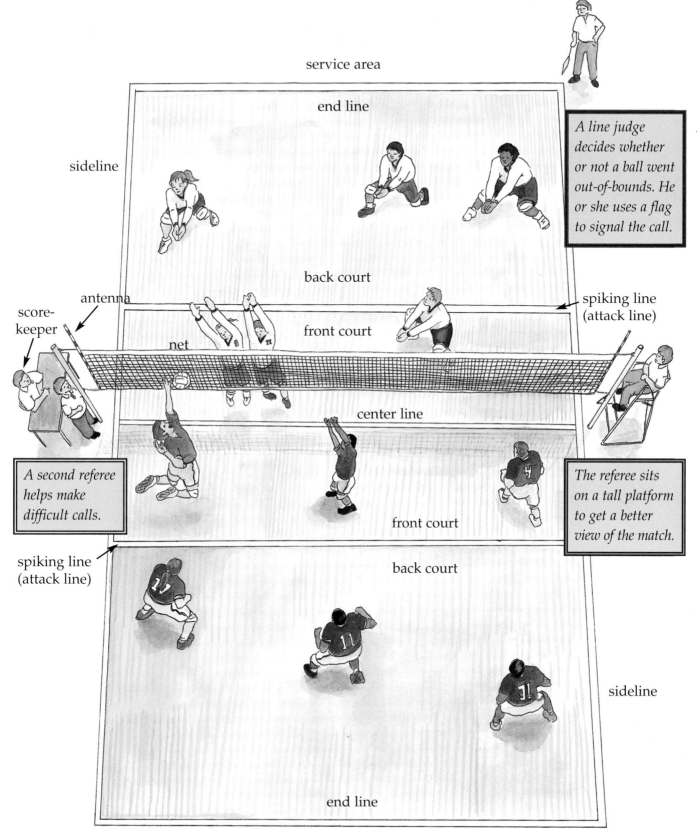

service area

end line

sideline

back court

antenna

score-keeper

spiking line (attack line)

net

front court

center line

front court

spiking line (attack line)

back court

sideline

end line

service area

The Essentials

Volleyball requires few pieces of equipment. You need only a net, ball, knee pads, and comfortable clothing. Unlike sports such as hockey or football, volleyball is not a contact sport. Players do not have physical contact with one another so they do not need a lot of protective padding.

Volleyball players wear a team uniform. Each player has a number to help the referees identify him or her.

A loose T-shirt allows a player to move easily while chasing and hitting the ball. Some players wear a long-sleeved shirt to protect their forearms.

Snug-fitting shorts allow a player to move around the court freely and easily.

The ball

A volleyball is made of an air-filled, rubber bladder that is covered with soft, padded leather. The bladder makes the ball light and helps it bounce. Leather padding makes it soft to hit with your bare hands and arms. You can practice with a volleyball that is designed for beginners. These balls are smaller and lighter than regular volleyballs.

Protect your knees

Players often must dive when reaching for the ball. **Kneepads** protect your knees when you drop to the floor while trying to contact a low ball. Stretchy material wraps around the back of your knee and holds the thick pad in place over your kneecap. Some players also wear elbow pads for protection if they fall when hitting the ball.

kneepads

Court shoes

Volleyball players wear lightweight court shoes. Court shoes have rubber soles designed to grip the floor as you move from side to side. Short, quick movements are hard on your ankles so choose shoes that are comfortable and have good support to help prevent ankle injuries.

Water supply

When playing sports, you will sweat and lose moisture. Keep drinking fluids to replace the water lost by sweating.

Warming Up

It is important to stretch your muscles and warm up your body before you play any sport. Stretching helps you get ready to jump high, bend easily, and run fast.

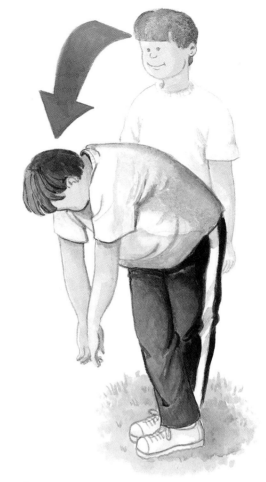

Arm circles

Stand with your feet shoulder-width apart and swing your arms in giant circles. Continue making circles in the same direction with each one smaller than the last. Keep going until your arms are out to your sides, and you are making tiny circles. Now switch directions— start with small circles and finish with big ones.

Leg crossovers

Stand and cross your legs at the ankles. Reach down slowly to touch your toes. Bend your knees slightly. Stretch as far as you can do so comfortably. Hold for five seconds, then switch legs. Do five stretches on each leg.

Trunk circles

Place your feet shoulder-width apart, and put your hands on your hips. Keeping your feet flat on the ground, swing your hips around in circles. Do three circles to the right and three to the left.

Neck circles

It is easy to hurt your neck so do this stretch carefully. Stand with your feet shoulder-width apart. Keep your chin tucked toward your chest, and slowly roll your head from side to side.

Leg lunges

Spread your feet apart as far as you can. Lunge by bending one knee and keeping the other leg straight. Rest your hands on your bent knee or the ground and count to five. Do five lunges on each side.

Points and Service

One team serves, or hits the ball to begin the rally. In most leagues, only the team that has service can score points. It is awarded a point if it wins the rally. When the receiving team wins the rally, it is awarded a **side-out**, which means it gets to serve the ball and has a chance to score.

Everyone can score

The rules are different in international competition. Teams can score points whether they are the serving or the receiving team. The first four games go up to 25 points and the last game goes to 15.

Keep on moving

Each team has a **serving rotation**, which is the order in which the players take turns serving. When your team wins a side-out, your team rotates in a clockwise direction. In the diagram to the right, each position is numbered from one to six to show the serving rotation. The serving position is number one. The player who will serve next is number two. Your coach or team captain tells the referee your team's serving rotation.

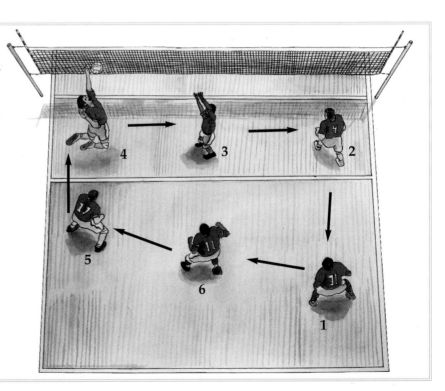

Before every serve, your team must be positioned in the serving rotation. If your team is out of order, the referee may give your opponents a point. After the ball is served, the players may move freely around the court.

Serving

There are several types of serves, including the **overhand** and **underhand** serves. The underhand serve is the easiest to learn. When you become confident with this one, try an overhand serve.

At your service

When a player serves the ball, he or she must stand behind the end line. You can serve from anywhere behind the end line, but you cannot touch or cross it until you have hit the ball. Courts used to have a marked service area; however, serving is no longer restricted to this area.

Stay in the lines

All serves must travel over the net without touching it. The ball must land inside the side and end lines. If it goes outside the lines, it is a **fault** and the other team is awarded a side-out. If the serve lands inside the lines without an opponent touching it, an **ace** is called and the serving team receives a point.

Wall ball

You can practice your serves against a wall. Stand four giant steps away, serve the ball, and then catch it when it bounces back. After you can catch three in a row, take a giant step back and serve again.

Concentration and focus are important when serving. This player keeps her eyes on the ball as she serves and does not let anything distract her.

Underhand serve

Hold the ball in front of you in the palm of one hand. Pull your other arm straight back. Keep your eyes on the ball.

Gently toss the ball up and swing your hand forward to hit it with the **heel** of your hand, which is just below your wrist.

As your arm swings forward and hits the ball, let your body weight shift forward. The heel of your back foot should lift off the ground.

Overhand serve

Hold the ball in the palm of one hand. Have your other arm raised about shoulder height above the ball.

Draw your raised arm back and toss the ball straight up. Extend your arm fully to hit the ball at the highest point you can reach.

As the ball comes down, swing your arm forward in a circular motion. Strike the ball with the heel of your hand.

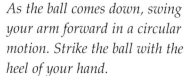

Returning the Ball

A team can hit the ball up to three times before sending it back over the net; however, one player cannot hit the ball twice in a row. When receiving a hit, most teams use all three hits—two to get the ball under control and the third to make an attack over the net. They often follow this pattern—**bump**, **set**, and **spike**.

The bump

Your opponents will try to hit the ball hard and fast over the net. The bump is used to slow down the ball so that your team can gain control of it. A **dig** is a diving bump used to hit a low ball.

The set

The second shot in the three-hit pattern is the set. The set is a hit called a **volley**. A volley sends the ball in a high, slow curve that makes it easy for a teammate to hit the ball over the net.

The spike

The spike is a hard, fast hit that shoots the ball toward your opponents' court. Players jump up when spiking to smash the ball while it is above the net. Spiking takes a lot of practice.

Different strokes

Not all returns follow the bump, set, and spike sequence. Sometimes you can receive the ball with only a volley and then spike it. Other balls may need more than one bump before they can be returned. Remember that you must receive a serve with a bump or volley—never a spike.

*Players wait for serves in the **ready position**. They stand with their knees bent, their arms lowered and bent, and their head up.*

During a rally, players cannot always see where their teammates are when they are watching the ball. To avoid bumping into your teammates, shout out "mine!" or yell your name when you're going to hit the ball.

Bumping

An opponent has just spiked the ball and it's coming straight at you. Don't panic! In this situation, the bump is perfect. It will send the ball up high and straight for a teammate to hit. You can use a bump to receive the ball almost every time it comes over the net. It gives the **setter** plenty of time to get under the ball and make a volley.

Sometimes you will not have a chance to get underneath the ball to bump it—you'll have to dig for it! A diving dig can save the ball and get your team back on the attack.

Learning to bump

1. With your hands joined, reach your arms in front of you so that they form a "V." With one foot in front of the other, bend your knees and lean forward from your waist. Watch the ball.

2. Move so that your arms will be directly under the ball as it falls toward you.

3. Keep your arms stiff and allow the ball to hit your forearms. Just as the ball hits your arms, straighten your knees and lift your arms and upper body in the direction you want the ball to go.

Ask a partner to toss the ball to you so you can practice bumping. Bump the ball to your partner so he or she can catch it without letting it bounce.

In slow motion

To perfect your bumping motion, practice with a balloon. It moves much slower than a ball. Toss the balloon up in the air. Grip your hands together, and move under the balloon so you are ready to bump. Bump it straight up in the air and catch it before it falls to the ground. Bump the balloon as many times in a row as you can before it bounces. Now try these drills with a volleyball.

Put your hands together!

Put your hands in each of these positions to find the one that feels most comfortable for bumping. In each position, your thumbs should be on top, side by side, and pointing forward.

1. Make one hand into a fist and wrap the other hand around it.

2. Lay one hand inside the other with the palms pointing up.

Volleying

Your teammate has bumped the ball, but it still isn't in a good position in which it can be spiked easily over the net. You need a slow, soft, and accurate pass to get the ball ready for a spike. You need a volley! Players use the volley most often.

The player on the left is the team's setter— she prepares the ball to be spiked. She aims her volley near the net so that a teammate can easily spike it.

Making the volley

1. Move under the ball. Bend your knees and raise your hands in front of your forehead with your elbows out to the side.
2. Form a **volley window** with your hands by making a diamond shape with your thumbs and index fingers. Keep your thumbs pointed slightly back toward your eyes.
3. As the ball reaches you, volley it by straightening your legs, then your elbows, and finally by pushing the ball into the air with your fingers and a flick of your wrists.

Get a grip

Try this drill to get a feel for flicking the ball when volleying. Do not catch the ball. Make the volley window with your hands and pick up the ball. Use this grip to bounce the ball on the floor. Be sure to push the ball off your fingertips and thumbs when you bounce it.

Volley wall

Throw the ball high against a wall and get ready to volley. Volley the ball hard enough to make it bounce back to you. Don't let the ball touch the palms of your hands. Try to keep volleying the rebounds against the wall without catching the ball.

This player is leaping to get under the ball in order to volley it to her teammate.

Spike!

The ball has just been set up in the air beside the net. You take a couple of steps, jump up into the air, and smack the ball down over the net. It moves so fast that your opponents can't stop it, and it smashes against the floor. Nothing scores points like a well-aimed spike!

A good spike takes balance, so your timing needs to be just right. If you are right-handed, make the first of your three approach steps with your left foot. If you are left-handed, begin with your right foot.

Fancy footwork

With a friend, you can practice these steps for spiking. Have your partner stand on a chair and hold the ball up and out to his or her side.

1. Stand three giant steps away. Approach as though you are going to spike the ball—step, step, and jump.
2. For the first few attempts, simply jump up and touch the ball. Allow yourself to get a feel for jumping at the right time.
3. Once you have control of your approach, spike the ball from your partner's hand. Your partner can also lightly toss the ball just before you spike so you do not hit your partner's hand.

Up, up, up

To hit a strong spike, you need to jump up so that your hand is as high or higher than the net. To jump that height, start a few steps back from the net.

1. Take one big step toward the net and the ball. Pull your arms down and back.

2. Take two smaller steps to help you jump into the air with both feet. Raise your arms, pulling your spiking arm up and behind your head with your elbow bent.

3. You want to hit the ball at the highest point of your jump. Swing your arm forward and smack the ball with the heel of your hand. Snap your wrist forward to send the ball shooting downward.

4. After finishing the spike, remember to pull your hands away from the net. If you touch the net at any time during the spike, you will lose the ball or a point.

*A **tip**, or **dump**, is a shot that is used to fool the other team. Jump up and raise your arm as though you are going to spike the ball hard. Instead of spiking it, however, lightly push the ball with your fingertips and hit it gently over the heads of your opponents. If used occasionally, the tip can fool the other team and score a point.*

Put it all Together

When you are learning to bump, volley, and spike, you can take your time and practice each skill on its own. In a game, however, the pace is faster. You will need to decide which shot to use in a matter of seconds. You will also have to know how to play as part of a team. These drills will help you learn how to play and cooperate with a teammate.

This team's setter and spiker have communicated well. The ball is in exactly the right spot to be hit.

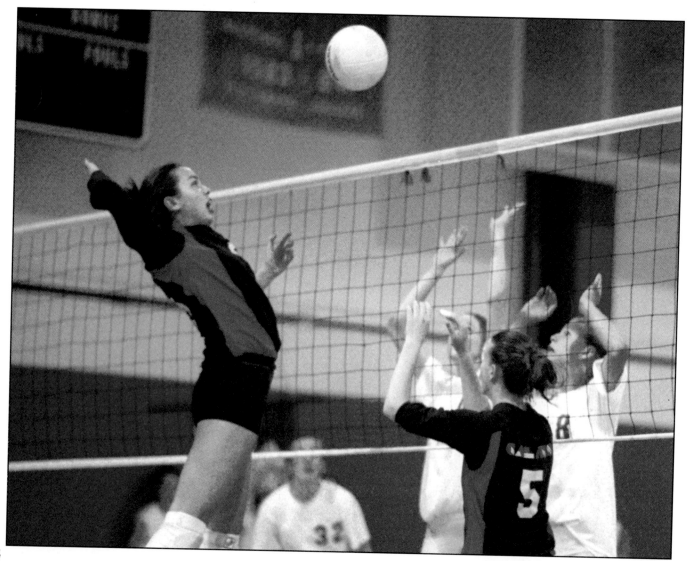

Mix and motion

The drill shown right uses two skills—bumping and volleying. Toss the ball straight up in the air, move under it, and bump it straight up. Now move under the ball and volley it straight up. Continue hitting the ball up, switching between bumping and volleying. You will learn how to position yourself quickly for different hits.

Three-hit drill

To practice the three-hit pattern, have your partner toss the ball high in the air. Get under the ball and bump it toward your partner. Now your partner volleys the ball to set you up for a spike. Run, jump, and spike your partner's volley. Switch places and do the drill again. Try tipping the ball sometimes instead of spiking it.

Tough toss

Have your partner toss a high ball to one side of you. It should be a few steps away from you. Run to the ball, get under it, and volley it back to your partner. Then have your partner toss the ball to the other side. Run and bump the ball back to your partner. To make this drill more difficult, have your partner throw low balls or balls that you have to run farther and faster to hit.

Blocking

Blocking the ball is a useful skill. A good block turns your opponents' spike against them. Almost as soon as it is spiked, the ball bounces off you and flies back to the other side of the court. Two or three players often block together to form a wall at the net.

It's not a hit!

When blocking, you do not strike the ball—it just bounces off you. For this reason, blocking does not count as a hit. If a block does not stop the ball at the net, your team still has three hits to get the ball to the other side.

Blocking basics

Blocking is all about skill and timing. While waiting to block, watch the other team's spiker. You want to time your jump so that you leap a split second after he or she does. This way your jump will be at its highest point as the spiker smashes the ball.

1. If you can, take a three-step run before you jump—it will help you jump higher. Most often, however, you won't have enough time. Instead, you will have to jump up and block from a standstill. Have your arms out to your sides, ready to reach up.

2. As you jump, reach both arms up as high as you can to block the ball. Remember, your hands cannot push or catch the ball. You can only have it bounce off you and down into your opponent's court.

Block bounce

Have a partner throw a ball high enough so that you must jump to reach it. Jump up and let it bounce off your hands or arms. Repeat this exercise ten times.

Jump, but don't touch

If you are alone, the best place to practice blocking is near a wall. Pretend the wall is a net and jump straight up, reaching your arms above your head. Jump as close to the wall as possible without touching it.

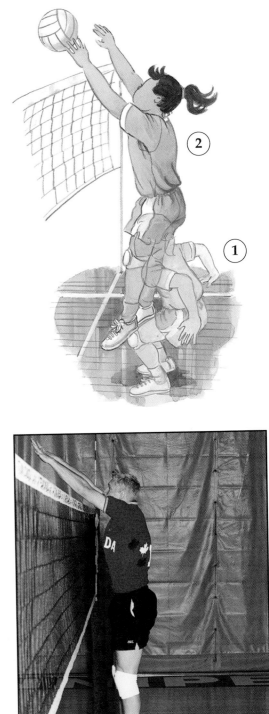

You are allowed to reach over the net while blocking. Be careful not to touch the net!

Faults and Penalties

The rules of volleyball help make the sport challenging and safe. Officials make sure the game is played fairly. When you break a rule, you have committed a fault. Officials punish faults with **penalties**.

What is my penalty?

If you get a penalty while your team is serving, the other team is awarded a side-out and gets to serve. If you get a penalty while your team is receiving, then the other team gets a point.

This referee is watching closely to be sure that neither team touches the net. The only people who can speak to the referee about his or her decisions are a team's coach or captain.

Take my card

Volleyball has rules that help control the players' manners. Players cannot be rude or disrespectful to other players or officials. The referee uses a **sanction** to punish a player for behaving poorly. The referee uses either a verbal warning, or yellow or red card to indicate the sanction. There are four sanctions:

 **Warning**: for minor offenses such as delaying a game accidentally. A second warning gets you a penalty.

 Penalty: for stronger offenses such as trying to distract an opponent. Penalties are also given for faults.

 **Expulsion**: for extreme behavior such being rude to opponents or officials. The player must sit out for one game.

 **Disqualification**: given to a player who sat out one game and then commits another extreme offense in the same match. That player must sit out the rest of the match.

*If you touch the ball twice in a row you have committed a fault called a **double touch**. If the double touch happens accidentally while you are trying to return a fast spike, shown above, the referee may excuse it and not call a fault.*

It's my fault!

Here are some of the most common errors that will cause you to be called for a fault:

- you allow the ball to touch the floor
- you hold or throw the ball
- you touch the ball twice in a row
- your team hits the ball more than three times in a row
- you touch the net
- your team is not in its serving rotation at service
- you cross the center line
- a serve is not performed properly

Beach Volleyball

Not all volleyball matches are played on an indoor court. Volleyball is often played on grass in parks and backyards. The most popular outdoor version of volleyball is beach volleyball.

It takes two

When people first started playing volleyball on sandy beaches, the rules were the same as the indoor game. Now beach volleyball has its own set of rules. Each team has only two players who cover the court. The court is not divided into a front court and a back court. As in indoor volleyball, players are allowed only three hits to get the ball over the net and cannot double touch the ball.

Not just for beaches!

Beach volleyball has become so popular that many clubs and resorts bring in sand to set up a court. By the time it became an Olympic sport in 1992, people were taking this type of volleyball seriously. Some players prefer beach volleyball because each player gets to hit the ball more often. Today, teams from all over the world compete against one another.

Volleyball Words

ace A serve that lands within the lines without being touched by the other team

attacker A player who is playing in the front court

attack line The line that divides the front court and back court

back court The area between the attack line and the end line

dig The act of diving to hit a low ball

double touch Hitting a ball twice in a row

end line One of two lines at the end of the court

fault An illegal move or play

free zone The area outside the side and end lines of the court

front court The area between the attack line and the net

line judge An official who identifies balls that are hit out-of-bounds

match A competition consisting of three or five games

rally The act of hitting the ball back and forth over the net

sanction A punishment given by the referee to a player for illegal behavior

serving rotation The order in which a team's players serve

setter A player who specializes in setting the ball

sideline One of two side boundaries on the court

side-out The transfer of service from one team to another after the serving team loses a rally

substitute An extra player who waits on the bench to play; also called a sub

tip A soft hit used to push the ball lightly over an opponent's reach

Index

1 2 3 4 5 6 7 8 9 0   Printed in the U.S.A.   8 7 6 5 4 3 2 1 0 9